The Tree in the Mind

Also by Ronald Moran

Poetry (Books and Chapbooks)

The Jane Poems
Waiting
The Blurring of Time
Diagramming the Clear Sky
Saying These Things
Greatest Hits, 1965–2000
Fish Out of Water
Getting the Body to Dance Again
Sudden Fictions
Life on the Rim
So Simply Means the Rain

Criticism

Four Poets and the Emotive Imagination (with co-author)
Louis Simpson

The Tree in the Mind

Ronald Moran

Copyright 2014 by Ronald Moran
ISBN 978-0-9890826-5-5

Published by Clemson University Press in Clemson, South Carolina

Editorial Assistant: Jessica Simpson

Cover Designer: Ellen Marley Yates

To order copies, please visit the Clemson University Press website: www.clemson.edu/press.

Contents

ACKNOWLEDGMENTS VII
DEDICATION IX

Part One

The Tree in the Mind 2
Silent Time 3
The Secret 4
Plantings 5
Urban Sprawl 6
Rapture 7
The Shenandoah Valley 8
Dry 9
Labor Day 10
September 12
Water 13
The Ice Pond 14
Auggie 15
Landing Pattern in Mid-Afternoons 16
The Doctrine of Fair 17
Life Inside a Window 18
This Is the One Night 19
Fifty and Married 20
Backward from Midnight 21
Crossing Boundaries 22

Part Two

A Corridor of Dreams 24
Patterns 25
Dream Makers 26
When Night Becomes Day 27
Sleep 29
The Final Dream 30
Dead Before His Time 31
Recalibrations 33
A Life Not Yet Led 35
This Year Beyond Others 37
On My 75th Birthday 39
End Zone 40
The Birthday Card 41
One Man's Saturday 43

One Man's Sunday 44
Lunch Downtown 45
Chairs 46
Burning Down to Ashes 47
Beefeaters on the Rocks 48

Part Three
Jimmy Sikes 50
Lobstering in Long Island Sound 51
New Britain, 1952 53
Legacy of a Coach 54
The Interview, 1958 55
Stories 56
Wasps 57
Your Dream and Mine 59
Chardonnay, David Kirby, and the Cheneys 61
On Using Both Hands 62
My Father in the Night 63
The Man Riding Next to Me 64

Part Four
Pollination 66
Declarations 67
War Comes Home, Week after Somber Week 68
Picture of a Soldier 69
Sonnet for a Dead Crow 70
After Reading a Novel Where the Women Fantasize about a Hunk on TV 71
Billy Storey 72
Würzburg in September 73
Young Death in China 75
A View from Here 76
Suppose the Return of Christ 77
Last Letter to Jane 78
The Final Reading 79
The Last Poem 80

A Note on the Author 82

Acknowledgments

Grateful acknowledgment is made to the editors of the following publications in which many of these poems appeared, some in slightly different versions.

Abbey: "Chairs," "Forecast for Colorado," and "This Is the One Night"

The Asheville Poetry Review: "Rapture"

The Blue Hour: "Burning Down to Ashes" and "My Father in the Night"

Chiron Review: "Billy Storey" and "Picture of a Soldier"

The Dead Mule School of Southern Literature: "Chardonnay, David Kirby, and the Cheneys," "Life Inside a Window," "On My 75th Birthday," and "September"

Evening Street Review: "End Zone," "Jimmy Sikes," "The Man Riding Next to Me"

Iodine Poetry Journal: "Dream Makers," "Dry," "The Last Poem," "A Life Following the Life," and "Water"

Loch Raven Review: "Beefeaters on the Rocks"

The Louisiana Review: "Stories"

The Main Street Rag: "Sonnet for a Dead Crow"

The Meadowland Review: "The Tree in the Mind"

The Orange Room Review: "A Corridor of Dreams," "Labor Day," "Last Letter to Jane," "Lobstering in Long Island Sound," "Patterns," "Recalibrations," and "Würzburg in September"

The South Carolina Review: "Auggie," "One Man's Sunday," "Pollination," "The Secret," "This Year Beyond Others," "Urban Sprawl," "A View from Here," "War Comes Home, Week after Somber Week"

Tar River Poetry: "One Man's Saturday" and "Silent Time"

This Week's Events at Malaprop's Bookstore/Cafe: "The Shenandoah Valley"

The Thomas Wolfe Review: "Crossing Boundaries"

The Wallace Stevens Journal: "The Interview, 1958"

Wild Goose Poetry Review: "After Reading a Novel Where the Women Fantasize about a Hunk on TV," "Backward from Midnight," "Declarations," "The Doctrine of Fair," "The Final Reading," "Landing Pattern in Mid-Afternoons," "Legacy of a Coach," "A Life Not Yet Led," "Lunch Downtown," "New Britain, 1952,"

"Sleep," "Suppose the Return of Christ," "Wasps," "When Night Becomes Day," "Young Death in China"

"Dead Before His Time" was previously published in *The Best of Poetry Hickory* (Main Street Rag Publishing Company, 2012). "The Tree in the Mind" was reprinted in *The Best of Poetry Hickory* (Main Street Rag Publishing Company, 2013).

"Crossing Boundaries" was read at The Thirty-Second Annual Meeting of the Thomas Wolfe Society on May 29, 2010.

"Burning Down to Ashes" was reprinted in *The Blue Hour Anthology: A Collection of Poetry, Prose and Art*, Volume II. 2013.

Dedication

In memory of my father, Ronald W. Moran (1901–1971), and my mother, Julia M. Moran (1906–1973).

Part One

The Tree in the Mind

The tree in the mind of the forest is different
                from
the tree in our minds, a psycho-philosophical
                notion
of drawing our own tree while trying to copy
                the tree

before us, but the tree in the mind of the forest
                must
grow and flourish while it becomes a fraction
                of the mind
of the forest, which is huge and, of course,
                profound

in its molecular composition and its collection
                of both ripened
and immature organisms, so that its center is
                unimaginable—
whether given in geological or geographical
                coordinates—

and where the detritus of a disruptive age
                would stare,
at us, as if we were interlopers in the forest,
                a privileged
renaissance of growth and decay, a sequence
                without end

Silent Time

The car is a hybrid and when it glides
                    into
my driveway, I do not hear it, even
                    when
I am sitting in my den, which faces
                    the stoop

on which all activity is abundantly
                    clear
in the den, since the walls are made
                    of cardboard,
but the driveway, now that's different:
                    concrete,

no trees to blur the sound of new tires,
                    which is how
it will always be. The world is becoming
                    silent, not still,
faster but more silent, so the parks have
                    been reclaimed

by pigeons or birds with better hygiene,
                    and out there
the silence of small children deadens
                    the soft air
of any season, while inside, their hands
                    manipulate

the future, in front of screens so alive
                    they tingle;
and in the open marketplace thin coils
                    of insulation
pretend to separate living from dead.
                    Hardware stores

sell plugs that look like ear muffs, No, like
                    earphones,
as if, Yes, you are talking to a good friend
                    about
maybe the chances of the Braves this year,
                    maybe.

The Secret

What follows is only what you know to be
                secret;
you will not tell anyone, even yourself out
                loud,
for fear that someone might hear what
                happened

and what you are planning to do about it,
                when all
you really want to say to them is *Nothing*, not
                because
you are offended by their curiosity, but, *No,*
                you do not

know what to do—whether *this* means good,
                to a point,
or bad, or, as the poet William Stafford once
                wrote,
somewhere in the band of mild sorrow, much
                closer

to the truth than some of what we want to say,
                and so,
it becomes, at first, a word buried in your tomb,
                until later
someone, maybe a grandchild, asks his mother,
                Did my

Papa do it and why didn't you tell me? To which
                she replies,
either by dropping her head or leaning her head
                back
with a smile, before she asks her child, *Why*
                honey,

where did you come up with this notion? And
                she replies,
I just know, and whatever side of this coin turns
                up,
the secret of *this* begins to share its intimate
                life.

Plantings

Here they come, awakenings of early May:
                first
promises, then the inexorable excuses why
                peach trees
fail to bud or why our finely caressed soil
                rejects

the history of its phylum, whatever shape
                it takes
this year, different, of course, from last year,
                and
sad, destructive. Hey, not all of us can be
                natural

landscapers or horticulturists, or even know
                beyond
what they teach at Ace Hardware, or, more
                seriously,
at Lowes or Home Depot, and so we admit
                failings

and, hence, try to profit from them, as if our
                plantings,
like children, will someday mature into whole
                beings,
healthy and, as they say, ripe for the picking,
                and how

we love our first harvest, a virgin festival, pure,
                ready,
and tender, and how we pray all future harvests
                will bear
the same for us, year after year, thus absolving
                us.

Urban Sprawl

Another late afternoon, the air thick with
            portents
of torrential rain, hail, floods, and perhaps
            a tornado
or two when ice and fire meet in the sky,
            and this

is only June, a placid month for us in upper
            state SC,
maybe a thunderstorm now and then but
            hardly ever
the potential for destruction, displacement,
            or death,

so we rely on radar from the local or national
            news,
or our own vulnerable computers to give us
            ample
warning of what to do in the case of violent
            weather,

but now I look out the four-pane Palladian
            window
in my den, and I see the leaves of my oak
            twitching
in the indifferent wind, a false negative, who
            knows?

given the corridor we live in, mountains to
            the north,
foothills to the south, and between them
            urban sprawl,
willing to take on anything to clear a buck,
            anytime.

Rapture

I am looking out a large window in the breakfast
                room
of my daughter's house on Lake Keowee, where
                any way
I turn, the only striking constant is the rapt notice
                I give,
every time I visit here, to the view where nothing
                changes,
except seasonally, and where I am compelled
                each time

to ask, *How much more will I be able to tolerate?*
                Of course,
I know there are equal views and, doubtless, even
                more
engaging ones, but I claim this one and I cannot
                let it go,
not yet, maybe never, and it is not like a picture,
                or any
reproduction, which must be finite and given,
                like all art.

The Shenandoah Valley

Through a four pane, small Palladian window,
                I see wisps
of clouds race, like sailboats, on a light blue sky
                in late

January, upstate South Carolina, where it is
                crisp and cool.
The clouds are racing against the Blue Ridge,
                and they know

they will lose, but this is a chance of a wintertime,
                and why not
take it, why not ride the wind up to North Carolina,
                into Virginia,

as far as the Shenandoah Valley will permit them?
                I remember
a dream I had over fifty years ago, to live there,
                in the valley,

mountains that could be tamed on either side,
                a rich
heartland in between, and the lifelong promise
                of love.

DRY

Sunday afternoon, like a tether without a boat,
                    or driftwood,
its name, always moving but never anywhere,
                    so it is

this July afternoon in upstate South Carolina
                    where water
is like money, where the bugs and spiders
                    have quit,

and lay dying or dead on stoops and decks,
                    the webs,
between bushes empty but for the detritus
                    of heat.

Even birds and squirrels have vanished or,
                    like other forms,
they just gave up. The silence is not so much
                    eerie outside,

as it is a message with a source, a visible sign,
                    as in,
Do Not Enter, Keep off the Grass, No Trespassing,
                  Keep Out.

Labor Day

Labor Day and I am doing what I do every day,
                nothing,
as if the decree of rest from labor applies to me
                this day,
when summer in the Northeast is officially
                over,
and tomorrow the nation begins, some areas
                quicker

than others, its fall mourning process, as in
                pharmacies
putting up signs advertising flu shots, school
                classrooms,
barely underway, teaching lessons in the art
                of contagion,
and the natural world, what is still left of it,
                playing

its penultimate anthems to life in death,
                distracting us
from the light that diminishes and the look
                of losing
on the faces of drivers at stoplights, of runners
                in their
own mini-marathons, while the wind chill
                factor

pitches its earliest hardballs striking like rockets,
                our chests
heaving, breaths coming quicker and harder;
                but, hey,
what about the other distractions: calls made
                by
brilliant quarterbacks; catches from another
                world

by wide receivers, thin, incredibly fast, hands
                like glue;
baseball in its post-season Armageddon, like
                teams on
uneasy trestles over which the march of nations
                passes

gloriously; and, basketball, at whatever level,
                rewarding

quick feet, eyes, arms stretching to heaven,
                which,
although we will never attain, we beg them to,
                saying,
Go to it: block, pass, rebound, score like mythic
                gods,
while I am thinking, dumbfounded in my study,
                Go for it.

September

September again, month of changes unlike any
                      other,
with public schools bulging, as always, and, hence
                      our
calendar of diseases opening its morbid covers,
                      and
no more vacations, no more time having fun
                      spending what

little we have in this economy, and, finally,
                      cool air
from Canada, lowering temperatures and even
                      tempers,
in this month little recognized as being personal,
                      but rather
as a materialization of football, from high school
                      to pros,

while Major League Baseball, its players so tired
                      some
can hardly wake up without wanting to quit,
                      except
for those enormous salaries for just dressing,
                      and,
as pros, yes, they do and sign autographs, try
                      to boost

their batting averages, or other percentages,
                      or whatever
statistics guide their tenuous futures, while we
                      implore
them never to strike, to forget our huge stake
                      in what
they do, in their fields of play, however high,
                      for all of us.

WATER

I'm sitting, as usual, in front of my computer,
        screen blank,
looking at the blinds pulled more than half-way
        shut, keeping
out the glare of the snowfall four days ago, rare
        where I live
in upstate SC, like water jumping through hoops,
        and I am
thinking about water, its simplicity of makeup,
        as well as

its complexities of power to do what it does—
        such as
making sleet, snow—and how we fight, even
        kill
on its behalf, while it does what it does, often
        where
we make it go and when, accepting our orders,
        but
keeping its integrity intact, its composition
        simple.

The Ice Pond

There's a way through the woods to the old
                    ice pond
below the ice house without even a hinge or
                    pane
of glass left, but sturdy, as if waiting for them
                    to return,
to cut, drag, and store their spoils for summer,
                    its men
steeped in cold all year long, clothed in sawdust
                    or straw.

There's no fence or wall or stand of evergreens
                    enclosing
the pond, but now it will admit only the chosen,
                    and then
just to sit or stand on top of its narrow dam,
                    to watch
the brim below, as thick as an old farmer's hand,
                    the wide
banded perch in small schools, spindle shaped,
                    all waiting.

Auggie

So I get a call from this guy who wants to clean
                out the mix
of undergrowth in back of my house, where
                snakes

and other residents of my waste zone live
                with impunity,
since, well, nothing will go back there, except
                a lost,

four point buck, moving as if he were jumping
                hurdles,
getting as high as he can before calling undue
                attention

to his presence, and this guy, Auggie, who is
                only
afraid of poison oak, but not the inhabitants,
                is the only one

I know of who will go there, and now he stands
                in my thick,
uncertain undergrowth, saying, *Hey Ron, I do
                this for you;*

and, remember, South Carolina in the summer
                is known
for bites, both deep and on the surface, but
                bites,

nonetheless, and I need to have undergrowth
                removed,
trees dismembered, and my little piece of land
                civilized.

Landing Pattern in Mid-Afternoons

At the same time every school day afternoon
    while I am
in my den, as usual trying to decipher the secret
    of my
small, singular universe, shrinking every day,
    I wonder

if the big one is also shrinking, as some say,
    or expanding,
as most astrophysicists maintain—my not being
    practiced
in their arts, so I believe—and given findings,
    it is fast

becoming an art, since each piece, however small,
    is needed
to sustain life in the universe; and I am impressed,
    not uneasy,
but if I were younger, I would take physics more
    seriously,

so while I am reflecting, with far fewer synapses
    than before,
about creation, endings without biblical prompts,
    I hear
a sound like a 737 in a landing pattern overhead,
    and I rise

to look out the four pane, Palladian window over
    my expanse
of blinds, for a Southwest Airliner, a new carrier
    flying 737s
to our airport, big jets for us, but the sound comes
    from a school bus

downshifting on a gentle decline, below the only
    landing pattern
over my subdivision, carrying five or six children
    from Oakview,
while someone waits for each one, as if the bus stop
    were a gate.

The Doctrine of Fair

One word that lives on the rim is *fair,*
                as in
That's not fair, the first poster child
                of
the teenage years, and whether right
                or not—
whether *they* may be right or not—
                Well,

what and how does *fair* really mean?
                The fairness
of this or that act to a teenager, such as,
                Son
You're grounded for a month. No car,
                no cell phone,
no computer time, except at school;
                and so

the doctrine obtains throughout one's life,
                when he says
to her, after she lands the big promotion,
                Well, dear,
I'm glad for you, but really it's not fair
                that
I have to (and you make your own list
                of items

constituting the unfairness of her action,
                or his
during the NFL season or whatever seasonal
                addiction
holds him). Does fair figure in this formula?
                Is it
always the one feeling slighted while circling
                the board

and landing on *Go to jail?* Is it always unfair
                if you are
snubbed, left out, rejected, denied? Why?
                What about
your role in this panoply of responses?
                I am trying
to be fair, but to be fair I must understand,
                I must.

Life Inside a Window

Life inside a window is never what it seems
                    from
outside a window, no epiphanic slides of
                    truth,
as in that claim of peering in a glass door
                    and
finding the stuff for a novel a century ago,
                    and even
if a window swears its compounds are pure,
                    its
square inches equal to one's ordinary sight,
                    still

it remains a matter of how far and how deep,
                    as Frost said
of people standing on a beach, looking out
                    at the sea—
who cannot look out either far or deep—
                    unless, say,
one is looking in a car window at a scene
                    of passion,
where depth is just a matter of cubic inches,
                    and what
one sees in one side, one sees from another
                    and another,

a continuum like a transcendental number,
                    no repeats
but the same digits appear, disappear, a mix
                    of patterns
not patterns but resembling a sequence,
                    just as
when one looks closely at a speck on a tile,
                    one swears
that speck is alive and moving but it is not,
                    except
in the window of the mind, where it starts
                    all over.

This Is the One Night

This is the one night of pipes freezing and bulbs
popping, as if the birth of a geologic fingerprint
were about to leave its mark, as if to proclaim

the most feared event were about to occur,
and you and I would have to pay the interest
due on an investment made on behalf of us

so long ago no one remembers or cares, yet
is willing to take its bounty by any carrier, one
or more gratis bundles, like a rest stop open

all night or a fountain in the desert, or the haven
of the universe opening its doors to paradise
in the relentless night, the calm of good friends.

FIFTY AND MARRIED

When you're fifty and have been married
                half the time,
or been with the same person that long—
                albeit
improbably, since, well, one or the other
                without

a ring easily finds reason to leave, a simple
                act,
excluding the emotions, if there are any
                left—
anyway, you want a change, not necessarily
                of your mate

but, say, your residence, as in wanting to live
                on a lake
or on the coast or in the foothills, not high
                enough
so that snow and ice only complicate your life,
                but someplace

different, as in the lyrics of a hard rocker,
                or even
the sound of a poetry slammer, in a church,
                as a band
of seasoned musicians tries to follow her lead
                wherever.

Backward from Midnight

I am trying to flutter my syllables, like wings
                of nervous moths
at street lamps on intersections, but, maybe,
                I should

try arranging my lines differently, so as
                to give
them more room to breath hypnotically
                before

my alarm commences its litany of beeps,
                while
I count backward from midnight, and, O,
                how the rails

on this old (and nearly) condemned bridge
                on State 123
will burst into harmony, as if a bow from
                the spheres

crossed rails, and if not celestial sounds, then
                crepuscular,
to stir our black bears into a dance of frenzy
                and delight.

Crossing Boundaries
for Thomas Wolfe, 1900-1938

I am in my den, as usual, looking out the four-pane
                Palladian window,
and, with my eyes shut, I take down Donna's house
                and Ben's,
caddy corner from mine, both across the street,
                due North;
and there it rises, in a haze, the Blue Ridge range,
                sleepy,

as if having just awakened to this softening day,
                its shoulders
rounded, and I think it is going to turn over,
                when the haze
lifts, and history, that armchair storyteller, pokes
                its head
over Caesars Head, looks back over at Table Rock,
                settles back

into the drowsy afternoon, under vapor trails,
                a few cirrus,
content to serve as the guardian of the gates
                to the Carolinas,
North and South, this range that Wolfe crossed.
                And, wait,
what is that, there, look, yes, standing on a ledge
                stretching

his large arms, looking East and West, as if for
                a way
to leave, a man on a mountain, no, a giant whose
                words
named both time and space, as did no one else,
                and who
crossed boundaries and, in the process, redefined
                them.

Part Two

A Corridor of Dreams

It is a corridor of dreams that begins my mornings
        at four or five a.m.,
with a special cast of characters, the dead living
        among them,
in scenes or plays I would not write but I must have,
        unwittingly,
or else how could they mimic my inadequacies
        so precisely?

Sometime after five this erratic morning, I dreamed
        of a open jeep
across the street in a driveway, driven by a boy-child
        who knew
only how to coast down a steep hill, where the jeep
        ran over
a little girl walking with other little girls; and when
        I could not

get to her, I tried calling 911, my ancient phone
        attached
to a cord, the operator telling me, *I'm sure she is
        only depressed
and only needs an antidepressant,* so I screamed,
        Goddamn it,
*she may be dead or dying, and I cannot reach her,
        but Jesus,*

she doesn't need an antidepressant! Call EMS!
        Silence,
and the next voice I heard was myself trying to greet
        my new neighbors,
both of whom had colds, him tall and accomplished,
        and she,
a red-haired beauty, in a house I do not know,
        my clothes

and my sleeping soul both in shreds, and later,
        after
I woke up, I thought of Jack Nicholson, smiling
        broadly
at patients in the waiting room as he left the office
        of his
psychiatrist, saying to them *What if this is as good
        as it gets?*

Patterns

So, when I woke up this morning, I was talking
                out loud
to Jim Gaskin, one of my old bosses who has
                been dead
for years, saying, *What we need to do is to find*
                the source
of where these long legal pads are stored, maybe
                the bookstore.

It's been that way lately: I talk to someone from
                my past,
and then wait for an answer; and when I do not
                receive one,
I wonder first, then ask again, before I realize I am
                awake,
and many with whom I am trying to talk are dead,
                not

unlike other times, when I think my Jane is here,
                puttering
in the kitchen until it is spotless, no matter how
                bad she feels,
or I wonder if, maybe, she is in her stiff chair in our
                living room,
reading or writing long notes on birthday cards,
                while I am

still awake evenings, having drifted in and out,
                waiting,
as my life in its distant past tries to take over,
                and, hey,
each of those legal pads I found was covered
                with
words or diagrams, lines in very odd geometric
                patterns.

Dream Makers

My land phone continues to play dead in the kitchen,
                          ignoring
any self-serving merchants who call me, those saying,
                          Hi Ronald,
did you get our recent quote about your car insurance? or
                          equally subtly,

Have you thought of what it will be like for your family
                          when
your time comes? Have you planned for their time of grief?
                          Well, not exactly.
I suppose not, but I have a gravestone with my name etched
                          on it,

and any urn will do. They know I am not particular, just so
                          he urn
is not flowered, and they know my sentiments. But what if
                          I outlive
all of them—hardly the case—but suppose the airplane
                          they all take,

but for me, on a fall vacation to Cancun drops into the Gulf,
                          and an oil slick
cruising the Gulf closes in on them and, like a smog, clogs
                          their sweet,
healthy lungs, leaving me the master of my own destiny,
                          except for,

well, maybe the church, if it forgives me my omissions.
                          What else
have I done to congest my nights, to write scripts for my
                          dream makers,
gathering at the back of my brain nightly, plotting, always
                          plotting?

When Night Becomes Day

It is 6:45 in the morning, and the temperature
           should be
in the mid-to-upper 60s, a great relief from
           our
afternoon burnings in upstate South Carolina,
           where

I am living out my days alone in a small house
           built
wrong from the street, like a row house, put up
           only
if the backs of properties face the uninhabitable,
           like mine;

but all I am really thinking about is how to get
           back
to sleep, now being like the middle of night
           for me,
even though my dreams are taking on too much
           of the bizarre,

as in a pair of lions chasing my car, and me having
           to shove
one of them out the window, while my mother
           grows
more insane by the moment, and I have to yell
           at her,

when, alive, she was just shy and self-conscious;
           and,
Uh oh, I am on a golf course I thought I knew well,
           and, *Whoa*,
there's a green with two holes, as if for beanbag,
           while

I am wearing a light brown suit, as out of place here
           as I feel
on this course that I thought I knew, and there's
           Mother,
sane as ever, leaning far over and making a putt,
           looking

at me as if I were insane (*What are you doing here?*)
                      but now
I am thinking, why do I want to go back to sleep,
                      when, Jane,
I have mostly nightmares since you died, and why,
                      when

I awaken, am I often talking out loud as much as
                      two sentences
to my dreammates, before I realize it, and I think
                      of the time,
in your last months, when I was dreaming of trying
                      to punch

some guy threatening both of us, while, in fact, I was
                      punching
your small back in slow motion until you woke up,
                      saying,
Ron, what're you doing? Stop it! And I did, my fist
                      in mid-air.

Sleep

It's much easier now for me to get the fantods,
                         as in,
for example, when I hear my house cracking its
                         knuckles,
I hear it as someone trying to crack the lock
                         on my

back door, and, in a move of utter futility, I aim
                         my
pencil flashlight in that direction, then try to fall
                         asleep,
until I start a round of dreams in which the dead
                         of

my life return, and while I am trying to please
                         them,
which is impossible, as it was when they were
                         alive,
I wake up, my body tingling, my heart beat
                         elevated,

and so I drink two glasses of water, add a third
                         pillow
under my head, leave the light on for a couple
                         of minutes,
and wait for the miracle of water to cleanse
                         me.

The Final Dream

And I wish it were and so would you if you
                    were I,
all these years having to wake up shaking,
                    after
having nothing to justify one's dream life
                    being

in shambles, even guilt will not satisfy my
                    trying
to explain a painful incident that still gnaws
                    at my psyche;
but last night I dreamed of my two children
                    as puppies:

Sally as my collie when I was a child, Wes
                    as furry brown,
sensitive and good-natured as RD, the only
                    good thing
to come from Sally's first marriage; and
                    why was

I wearing a military uniform, without any
                    stripes
or medals, without my having ever served
                    our country
in the military, except for years in AFROTC?
                    And my Jane,

gone these four plus years, was herself,
                    calm,
at ease, the most normal one among us,
                    while
we tried to help somone else sell a house.
                    Who, why?

Dead Before His Time

I went to the bank today to cash a small check
                      and exchange
fifty ones for two twenties and a ten; and while
                      the latter
was not a problem—the ones being real and hence
                      verifiable—

the computer told the teller I was dead and, well,
                      so was
my joint account, since my wife died in February,
                      and the computer
said I died in April, and no one could override it.
                      Meanwhile,

as the line behind me grew longer and itchy,
                      I heard
someone mutter, *I wish he was dead,* to which
                      I replied,
I probably will be before this is ever settled.
                      The line

started snaking around a kiosk, and all the bankers
                      could say
was, *I can't override this. I don't have the authority.*
                      Silence, until
a teller from the drive thru, took my check,
                      initialed it,

and gave me my money, to a round of applause
                      from the line.
By the time I was leaving I was pretty mellow,
                      indeed,
laughing inside at the absurdity, not of the bank,
                      but of

our lives, how all of us clamber to be served
                      right now;
and when we're not, how we voice our feelings.
                      So, as
I weaved my way out among those in line, smiling
                      when I could,

I saw the woman who had wished the computer
            was right,
and, in a playful mood, I pointed my index finger
            at her
and raised my thumb, as if I were holding a gun.
            She cried out,

He's got a gun and passed out, falling directly
            into the man
behind her, who also fell back, with one after
            another,
going down, as if they were obeying orders
            from

George "Bugs" Moran; and as they collapsed
            into one
another, someone behind the tellers' booths
            hit the alarm.
Bells rang, doors locked, and you'd think,
            Hey,

this is the real thing, even before the cops came,
            weapons drawn,
blue lights flaring, the whole shopping center
            in a daze,
while I could not help but think, *Well, maybe now
            she'll get her wish.*

Recalibrations
for Sally

So now I had time for my surgery, thinking,
        Surely
this will be the beginning of something;
        and after
serving my term of rehabilitation, nothing
        was different

when I returned: the house stilled, Jane's
        decade
of illness and pain over, a prayer shawl
        folded
over the back of her wingback chair, no task
        at hand.

If anyone aware of my history—what passed
        for my passage—
asked, *What do you want to do now, Ron?*
        I said,
I want to have fun; and when my daughter
        asked,

What do you mean by fun? I was silent,
        since *fun*
was, after all, an emotive term with many
        referents,
and instead of deconstructing my answer
        to discover

an improved response, I just shortened it;
        hence,
I want to have, which was too skewed
        to describe
a new life, one recalibrated—now that's
        a good word—

when someone said, *You want to do what?*
        Which
only left, *I want to*, a brief, no-nonsense,
        forceful
intention; but unfulfilled, like a line drive
        hit right

into a glove. So here it is, stripped of all
                its potential,
I want, a wildly popular sentiment of most
                four-year olds,
who knew much better what they wanted
                than I did.

A Life Not Yet Led

So now it is official, the last quarter, no doubt
            to be
abbreviated, has begun in a flourish of notices
            in my mail,
offering clinics in hearing loss, urgent care,
            as well as

package deals for funerals, cemetery discounts,
            and, yes,
mostly ads for retirement villages, where
            a couple,
tanned and healthy, are smiling to a visual
            backdrop

of a white gazebo on a lawn sloping toward
            water,
a peaceful blue, the hint of a sailboat distantly,
            and, O yes,
the good life still before you, if you can afford
            to pay,

which I cannot, or else I would be there. And,
            why not?
I am living alone, and maybe now I should
            check out
the bargain basement villages, with one meal,
            two rooms,

700 square feet, one closet, a microwave,
            hot plate,
and all the water you can drink, inclusive,
            as if
on a vacation to St. Lucia after the seas rose
            on a tide

of global warming, leaving patches of dirt,
            some sand,
and all the guests huddling on high ground,
            waiting
for a helicopter, rowboat, trained dolphins,
            anything

to get them back to where they came from,
and refunds
for the life never led, but always promised
in the mail,
on the phone, online, and drawn in the sky
like clouds.

This Year Beyond Others

Not a time I thought I would be here, so I try
                to make
the best of it, but how I wish my limbs would
                obey
orders, but I did stumble into mildly truculent
                surf

at Hilton Head in recent weekends, and while
                I was
never over my head, I came close, as did my
                willing
companion, not a swimmer, and, yes, I watched
                her

despite the morbidity of my eyes, when, *Un oh*,
                by chance
I struck a jellyfish on patrol, scouting for its
                willing
companion, any one of the varieties of shark
                in this

upbeat area, slowly building up hunger during
                these
unproductive, hot days on the coast, hence
                obliged
to come closer to shallow, coastline waters
                on just

the remote chance of finding a sluggish meal
                without
beaching its body of steel, still calm, its sensors
                awake;
and if you have ever seen a fin in shallow waters
                between

you and friends, closer to shore, backs to the sea,
                you know
to be still and not shout to them what you see,
                but, slowly
tell them, one terrible syllable after another,
                Hey

*guys, turn your heads, not your bodies, and look
             behind you;
and when you go, go slowly, make no foam, noise,
             but before
you try, make sure its fin is heading out to sea,
             deep sea.*

On My 75th Birthday

So on this night, I must act as if others control
                    my actions,
as if I am unable to act for myself, not because
                    of any legal
maneuver, but because of a lemon I ate earlier
                    today

at a restaurant, not just a slice but, rather,
                    all of it,
tart and juicy, after waiting ten minutes
                    for
my iced tea to come; and what if a few other
                    customers

found it unusual that anyone would even think
                    to eat
a lemon whole, rind and all, in this posh venue,
                    and then
be happy? That's how I felt, no slur to service
                    or kitchen,

but I was thirsting for a lemon—its sharp, anxious
                    juice, flesh
on my ancient taste buds, surprising them, and
                    yes, what
joyous reaction, leaping to attention, this day
                    above all.

End Zone

What day is it, as if I am incarcerated, where
    perhaps
I should be, for lapses in attending to the needs
    of Jane,
as I think I should have near the end, when days
    lost
their calendar, except for light and dark, more
    of the latter,

I think, and when I bent to ask her, far deep
    into her
deepening sleep, *What do you want me to do?*
    she rose,
as if in a dream, defying all norms of a coma,
    and said,
Love me, before drifting back onto her bed.
    Silence.

How else could I love her but hold on to her?
    my cheek
resting on her dry cheek, her body temperature
    rising,
as if taking its last stand against dying, her mind
    already steeled,
against the idea of death, its corridors barred
    forever.

And even though I was absolved by an agent
    of time,
I cannot absolve myself from believing, Yes,
    I should
have done more, been calmer when she was
    confused
about what pills I laid out for her to take.
    What else

could I have expected from her? when so much
    was loosed
into her sweet system—Morphine, Neurotin,
    and she,
never complaining, accepted what befell her,
    and how
I wish I could have, too, but I gave up trying,
    too soon.

The Birthday Card

This year the only card I got on my birthday
                was from
a hearing center, offering specials, such as
                free workups
by licensed professionals, free consultations,
                and from

15 to 40% off on my preferred hearing aid;
                but since
I only have a miniscule hearing problem,
                I thought,
Well, why are they sending me a card?
                Also,

Why didn't they call me instead? Until
                I realized,
they think I am so hearing impaired that,
                if they
called me, I might respond with, *What?*
                I can't hear!

and on and on, so that the caller, perhaps
                untrained
in phone etiquette with the hearing impaired,
                would start
to speak louder, then, by progression, begin
                to scream;

and here we are, two people with not a thing
                against
each other, in a verbal war of explanation:
                hence,
the well wishes of a professional staff sent
                by card

to a man undeserving but happy nonetheless
                to be
thought of on his birthday, 77th at last count,
                with
the odds not much in his favor of another 10;
                but

as a woman once said to me, whenever I would
bring up
a maverick notion better left unsaid, unbridled,
You never know,
and she said it smiling and spirited, as if, well,
You never do.

ONE MAN'S SATURDAY

Since it is a Saturday again, I should do
                      something,
so I call up my 50-year-old twins, who
                      are always
busy, and that means I will check out
                      the news
on the Internet, and there she is again,
                      Paris Hilton,
this time arrested for possession of coke,
                      as smoke
from the sweet weed floated out of her
                      car
in Las Vegas; and while I am bemoaning
                      the media
for giving her such close coverage, I do it,
                      too—
the hypocrite, a widower on a Saturday
                      with
nothing to do in the afternoon but wait
                      for twilight,
when, yes, I will get into my car and go,
                      just go.

One Man's Sunday

So, when I try to bring up *One Man's Sunday,*
                a poem,
I wrote a short time ago, I only get a blank
                screen,
as if I never wrote the poem, so I am thinking
                Why?
Then I realize Why, because some glitch
                in my

new computer must have deleted it, and
                if so,
it is far gone from my being able to retrieve
                it, and while,
maybe not an immortal poem, but one still
                frozen
in the warm ice of my computer's memory;
                and so,

while it grows in value in my speckled memory,
                I think,
who is really to blame, and, naturally, only me,
                and so,
the poem is still lost, and I think, my cohort guilt
                saying
to me in its own very special way, *Hey, dumb ass.*
                How

could you possibly delete forever the next star
                of
the Pushcart Prize Anthology? So I ask, is that
                how
it is going to be in my last years— one more
                excuse
for failing to become, not what I am, but, well,
                what?

Lunch Downtown

I am in this restaurant with my daughter and granddaughter
                            for lunch,
and this server begins by telling us how he broke his glasses
                            this morning
and can see clearly only in the distance, a kid probably home
                            from college.

Now no one else can get another word in, ever since Sally,
                            my daughter,
had to ask him, *How did you break them?* Which, of course,
                            led
to a discourse involving something like flexible rims that one
                            can twist

like sticks of licorice; and, meanwhile, as I am trying to read
                            the menu
the letters seem to be leaning this way or that, and swooping
                            over
the menu like lost swallows on a flight back home. And then,
                            well,

I realize that I am confusing my vision with his, that somehow
                            in this
corner of the universe, I have actually empathized with someone
                            I do not
know, nor ever will, but our tracks have crossed some invisible
                            boundary,

like those that keep dogs in yards or old people in the home,
                            if only
momentarily, and so I listen more carefully, take my eyes off
                            the menu,
and nod sympathetically, as he now begins to recount his past,
                            passionately.

Chairs

I am sitting in my den with a backache,
                maybe
from reading too long in the squat chair—
                black leather,
with a lead base—that my father-in-law
                managed

to buy when one of the Fortune 500
                (Heublein),
after ordering the chairs for its Directors,
                reneged,
returning the chairs, and Fred struck gold.
                It's a tough

little chair, black leather and a look that one
                should not
cross it, so I have to sit on it or else, well,
                sometime
it could turn on me, like my garage steps
                that night

I tripped and the ironing board fell on me.
                I think
it's waiting for me to get out of this chair,
                the one
I use with my computer—so beat up it aches,
                as if

the black chair whacked it around one night
                out of
jealously or just its inherent mean streak.
                I think
I've already said too much, given the climate
                around here.

Burning Down to Ashes

I burned down to ashes once too often
for my age, advanced; but since blame,
like guilt, demands yet another lopsided
amount of our time, given cable news
networks, like Fox, setting programs
up on afternoons to be like prizefights,
I am trying to adjust my lone lifestyle
to be more harmonic, like the cooling

vibrations of my wind chimes that hang
down from the eave of my porch, caressing
each other so lightly you'd think they were
celestial, not a term to define our culture
or me, my singularity with self and wine,
until tonight, when I rose out of my ashes.

Beefeaters on the Rocks

During Happy Hour I was sitting at a bar drinking
        Beefeaters
on the rocks, with a splash of water, when a woman
        next to me,
mid-forties, I guess, very attractive and sensual,
        turned to me,

exhaling a long blue cloud, and said, *I like being wet*,
        to which,
I had nothing to say, not knowing what she meant,
        but thinking,
of course, as one might be conditioned to at a bar,
        maybe sex.

No, she can't be coming on to a bald 73-year-old,
        so I lifted
my glass, touched hers, and said *Prosit*, and we sat,
        until the good life,
or something similar, called her away and she never
        returned,

leaving behind a scent that titillated and aroused.
        I never saw
her again and never will, and I am wondering now,
        Did she speak
to me, or did I drift off momentarily, the fantasy
        of a man alone?

Part Three

Jimmy Sikes

Before I turned six, Jimmy Sikes would come to our
        back door,
asking, *Can Ronnie come out and bring his trucks?*
        according
to my father, who gave Jimmy a voice pattern foreign
        to me,

and I kept telling him, all through his life, *No, Dad,
        Jimmy
didn't sound like that at all*, and my father would
        only laugh,
dismissing me as of no account, since he answered
        the door

and knew. Not long after we moved five miles away,
        Jimmy died
in a house fire, and what difference did it make
        anyway
what Jimmy sounded like? But I wanted it to be
        right for Jimmy.

Who knows why we can't tab down to the next line,
        why something
sticks to our fingers and will not let go, even if it is,
        like Jimmy,
a presence so remote, so removed from us, forever,
        like a quasar.

LOBSTERING IN LONG ISLAND SOUND

I read a short piece in today's *Greenville News*
        about
the severe drop in lobsters in Long Island Sound,
        for reasons
not easily known, and I remember, when I was
        10 or 11,

going out on a lobster boat for the first, and sadly,
        the last time
of my life, in Long Island Sound, the boat owned
        by my uncle's
father, whose livelihood depended on lobsters;
        and that day

there was no reason to doubt that lobsters and
        the Sound
were companionable; and as I watched, I kept
        thinking
of my Uncle Oliver, boisterous, high-spirited, how
        he never

knew me well, and I believed, never thought highly
        of what
he knew of me, and what if, on a whimsy, he tossed
        me into
Long Island Sound, knowing I could not swim, while
        all

the crew were busy harvesting their traps, locking
        huge claws
with thin pieces of wood, hence making them docile,
        unable
to be a threat to anyone, as I watched, the terror
        of my

imagination growing magnificently, until we turned
        around,
heading home, the inboard churning with such noise
        and force,
the crew downing beers, ignoring their catch, happy
        the day

would soon close down, while I began to thaw out,
                my fears
as irrelevant as a stray porgy caught in the traps,
                and I stood
next to Uncle Oliver, smiling, relieved, thankful,
                O yes, thankful,

and yet I never told anyone of my irrational fears,
                fearful
they would either dismiss me with indifference or
                pretend
I said something so preposterous it did not need
                to be answered.

New Britain, 1952

I am reading a novel set in England toward
        the end
of the 19th century, where a woman of station
        says
to a much younger woman of no station,
        Forgive me
for saying so, but no woman of my class would
        wish

a man of her family to marry quite so far below
        him;
and I think of a time 50 years ago when I once
        took out
a girl below my middle, middle-class family
        who
was lovely and as nice as she was lovely, too.
        My

mother thought she was unacceptable, and
        at 16
I knew why, but that meant very little to me,
        since
I liked her—Polish background and long name,
        including
her living in a three family walk-up off Broad—
        but I knew

my mother, a Hungarian in disguise as a WASP
        with
her married name, would soon stare at me as
        she did
too often at my father, with that *No, No* look,
        saying
nothing, but we knew exactly what she meant
        then,

in New Britain, Connecticut, early 1950s, so
        I never
asked this lovely girl out again, but, O, what
        I missed;
how I wish I could say to her now, *I am sorry*
        Sweet girl,
with the bright eyes, white blouse, whose life
        I lost.

Legacy of a Coach

In my high school, the football coach taught
    gym,
and my senior year he made us stand, side
    by side,
the toes of our Keds on the out-of bounds
    line,
most wearing mismatched shorts and t-shirts,
    all misfits

he called us, because we did not play football
    and
thus had to take gym in the fall/winter term.
    He stood
at the vertex of his isosceles triangle, maybe
    some
thirty feet in front of us, caressing a softball
    like a lover,

while explaining his version of dodge ball:
    throwing it
hard as he could, at randomly chosen targets.
    Once hit,
if not already floored, we had to sit, nursing
    wounds
in silence, while the last of us standing, neither
    bruised

nor bloodied, to be rewarded by exempting
    gym
for the rest of the school year, with the grade
    of A.
As the coach wound up, as if he were pitching
    hardball,
we sat down, later calling it passive resistance,
    much later.

The Interview, 1958

While I was being interviewed by someone
                from Personnel
at the Hartford A & I Insurance Company,
                I asked him
(I had nothing to lose since I already blew
                the interview

by refusing the guy's offer of a cigarette
                and coffee,
my not seeming to be a frat-enough-type,
                and maybe
being a little too serious about what I thought
                mattered,

like reading), *Did you know Wallace Stevens?*
                He leaned forward—
his first movement of this already dead interview—
                Wally? Hell yes!
Then I said, as his butch hair cut seemed to grow
                before my eyes,

You know he wrote poetry? His second reply,
                Hell no?
You sure Wally wrote poetry? I'll be damned,
                while
I was thinking, I hope not, but, well, maybe
                he might.

Stories

Nothing going on inside my study or outside,
        and so
I think of this kid, about 18, in my second
        year
as a graduate assistant at LSU, in a freshman
        course,
who, when I gave the class an assignment
        to write

on something important that happened to them,
        came up
after class, first time ever—the semester being
        nearly over—
and said to me, *Mr. Moran. Nothing important
        has ever
happened to me,* and, in my incredulity, I said,
        Sure it has,

Come see me in my office; and after we talked
        45 minutes,
he was right: nothing important ever happened
        to him,
at least as far as he or I could interpret his life.
        I went home
to Jane and the twins, feeling as low as I ever
        had

in Baton Rouge, but I realized then, or shortly
        thereafter,
that, yes, something had happened but neither
        one of us
was skilled enough, both neophytes in different
        contexts,
to identify it or to be able to bring it out:
        since then

I always look at a class of students, thinking
        of the stories
they have to tell and how they, as storytellers,
        would grow;
and if I may never know what stories they have
        to tell,
they would blossom later, in the right season
        for them.

Wasps

I suppose, sometimes I did not control my
                actions
or demeanor or whatever separates mature
                adults
from students while I taught English full-time
                at
Clemson University, during a five-year period
                when
I held no administrative post to supplement
                my

salary and, hence, I must have thought I could
                act
like a goon with impunity in the safety of my
                office,
to free whatever demons were trying to run
                my life—
as common as it was then—which means
                little
to inner or outer demons, who relish our flaws.
                One spring

a swarm of wasps invaded the corner, eighth-floor
                windows
of Strode Tower, my home, and since the P Plant
                wanted
nothing to do with wasps, it was up to my buddy
                Harold,
whose office was next to mine, and me to find
                a way
to save us from the imminent threat of wasps
                occupying

our offices, thus cutting short our tenure, two
                almost
middle-age faculty with the world of literature
                before us,
so I took the lead, with Harold's concurrence,
                found
a wasp, dead on the floor, and taped it to one
                of the tall
leaky windows in my office, as if it were a cross,
                my version

of an omen I wanted the workers to convey
to
their Queen and, well, they were gone within
24 hours,
with no fanfare whatsoever, and Harold and I
resumed
preparing for classes, grading papers, meeting
with students,
none of whom ever knew the perilous threat
we averted.

Your Dream and Mine

> *This dream the world is having about itself*
> *includes a trace . . . .*
>   William Stafford

I am lying in bed sneezing every few minutes
                but never more
than twelve at a time, my own record broken
                easily
by Fred, my late father-in-law, whose count
                exceeded

at least fifteen, with a forty-second interval
                between each
(a medical wonder, I thought). The large
                paper bag
by the side of my bed fills up with Kleenex,
                while I am

listening indifferently to an AM station
                when, *Huh,*
I hear that last night someone removed
                the ATM
from Wachovia Bank on Woodruff Road,
                with a forklift.

Wait, isn't that the dream of everyone?
                to harbor
secretly but not to act on. All those crisp
                twenties
stacked there in the ATM, waiting to be
                lifted out

with impunity. I remember seeing a white,
                single-wide
trailer, a branch bank, one car usually
                parked
in front, somewhere in the rural Carolinas,
                in a field

by itself, without much vegetation, in a time
                before
Rush Limbaugh fabricated his Mt. Olympus
                to climb,

and Al Gore said he invented the Internet.
                    Whenever

we passed that way, I turned to say to Jane,
                    Let's toss
a lasso around it and drag it home, of course
                    revealing again
my secret—to which she only replied by rolling
                    her eyes.

Chardonnay, David Kirby, and the Cheneys

Now I am really loosening up: Chardonnay and reading
           David Kirby,
whose poems, I think, would make even Dick Cheney
           relax,
if ever he would read them, and now the question is,
           What

to do with myself? A soft body and a mind that once
           worked
when it was put to hard tests, but not nearly enough
           of them
to sustain the flow of synapses that weds one thought
           to another,

that wants to make one right and the other wrong,
           as in
a man I once knew who swore he had three eyes,
           and when
his best friend told him the truth—that his third eye
           probably

rolled back into his head—he killed him, saying,
           *He will
never doubt me again,* his trial becoming a classic in
           the tabloids,
and with its own moral, I guess, if I could see deeply
           enough.

I figure it's not worth it now, maybe never was, but I
           still think
of the friend and keep wondering what is safe to tell
           anyone
these days, and what do I mean by *these days?* Well,
           how are they

any different from those days or any other days in
           history,
except, of course, when some are more historic or
           histrionic
than others, and I know Lynne Cheney reads poetry.
           Does Dick?

On Using Both Hands

It's going on 10:30 p.m. and the tall kid up
                    the street
is shooting baskets. As usual, I am sitting in
                    my den,
and I hear him dribble several times, then
                    silence,

following by a louder bounce. Five, maybe
                    six years ago,
I watched him shooting baskets while I was
                    walking
in the neighborhood. He might have been
                    nine,

so I said to him, *Be sure you learn to dribble
                    and shoot
with both hands,* and I have not talked with
                    him since,
but I see he has long arms and legs, probably
                    plays

for his school or in some community league,
                    and, yes,
he dribbles and shoots with both hands, and
                    most
of the year he is on his driveway doing both,
                    which

reminds me of myself over 60 years ago, trying
                    to shoot
an oversized basketball that never fell through
                    the hoop
in my driveway on South Mountain Drive, me
                    having

always to punch the ball out the way it went in,
                    the reason
I tried to convince myself later, when it did not
                    matter,
why I never learned how to dribble or shoot
                    left-handed,

and, by extension, why I never learned how
                    to play
defensively, wanting only to shoot over and
                    over
until the ball went into the hoop and cleared
                    the net.

My Father in the Night

I woke up to the dark of early morning, no light,
        no splinters
of the moon poking through the blinds, wide
        awake,
when I saw my father, in color against a black
        backdrop,

from his waist up, older, as when he died,
        his face
tanned, as if he had been in the sun, his hair
        full, gray,
his eyes the only part of him moving, first
        toward me,

then from side to side, then down, a blanket
        on my
bed attracting him, as his image or presence
        began
slowly to dissolve, so I said, *You're fading, Dad,*
        my only words

after 40 years, while his dissolution continued
        like an object
disappearing in a whirlpool, and I was awake,
        as awake
as I ever was, but not alarmed or frightened or
        even

surprised, but powerless and saddened he had
        to leave,
however he came: from my mind because I had
        dreamed
of him earlier, or from where I could not know,
        not then.

The Man Riding Next to Me

The man riding next to me is my dead father.
He is sitting straight, his eyes on the road.
In his life, he could not teach me to drive—
our black Dodge lurching back and forth
down Cedarwood Drive, like a black bear

hurt in the hunt, my father more animated
than I had ever seen him, his childhood
stutter having returned, mocking him—while
I pumped pedals, as the rear end of our car
bounced like a rubber ball, and since I could

not understand anything he said, I gave up,
our car at peace, my limp arms draped over
the steering wheel, my father staring out
the side window at whatever was there,
so I said, *Why don't you drive home, Dad?*

Part Four

Pollination

Because of a bad toothache, I am driving
            to the dentist
on Haywood Road, down one of the very
            few hills
in my city. In the distance, instead of
            a blue mist
climbing up over the mountains near
            the beginning

of the Blue Ridge range in the Carolinas,
            I see
a yellow cloud bank, rising over half way
            up
the range: pollen, the poster child of where
            I live,
upstate South Carolina, with more varieties
            of growth

pollinating the air than anywhere else in our
            country.
Here, our home economy thrives on pollen:
            Kleenex,
face masks, allergy medicines selling like salt
            in a snow zone.
I turn my wipers on to clear the pollen off
            my windshield,

while in the dentist's parking lot, in mid-morning,
            cars sleep
under thin, yellow blankets. Big Business, too,
            for car washes,
and the people who work there—half afraid,
            half delighted
that they are here in the upstate, where
            the authorities

arrest speeders, not aliens washing cars or
            cutting lawns,
or working construction, what little there is;
            and the dentist
gives me an antibiotic, with a poop sheet
            that tells
about the drug that may, on rare occasions,
            kill one.

Declarations

So, if I want to declare something, a new trick
                    for me,
should I use Facebook or Twitter or should I try
                    to write
yet another poem, this time with more insistent
                    rhythms
than I am used to, and with end-stopped lines,
                    punctuated,

here and there, with different characters, as in
                    a dash,
question mark, exclamation point, period, and,
                    rarely,
a question mark, since almost all of the texts
                    on how
to write a poem discourage use of questions,
                    as if,

well, how can readers give a proper feedback?
                    And
what is sacred about a line being end-stopped,
                    as in
I hear the honking of a flock of Canadian geese.
                    Why?
Must they be lost because they honk? O, Yes.
                    I must stop

declaring, and why do I say, *if I wanted to declare,*
                    since
that is the province of those more confident, like
                    the young,
and why should I declare anyway, being neither
                    seer
nor prophet, nor talk show host, nor Cable TV
                    analyst?

War Comes Home, Week after Somber Week
Caption on MSNBC.com

Now that's a headline you don't want to read,
    not even
acknowledge in the enlightened 21st century, as
    I am sitting
in my den, as usual, watching an oak out my
    window

gesticulating like a child in distress, and I think
    I am
the only resident in our area not to condemn
    the oak
as gawky or maybe uncoordinated, like a child
    stricken

with a deficiency that, later, may or may not
    correct itself,
so the child, then grown, may have to be
    wheeled
everywhere, while the parents, worn down,
    apologetic

for nothing but consciously loving each other,
    innocents,
while their child will never function as an adult,
    which,
of course, might have meant his or her going
    to war

in the Middle East, perhaps even ending in
    a wheelchair
anyway, but sadder, more bitter, cursing
    VA hospitals,
which try but are always underfunded, like
    research

on autoimmune diseases, mainly for women,
    and now
all I want to know is this: When I asked Jane
    near the end
of her hard dying, *When is it ever going to end?*
    and she said,

Don't get so upset Ron, try to be more patient,
    dear,
Why did I go into the garage, get in the car,
    drive,
her life following me like a missile, cockpit
    flaring?

Picture of a Soldier
MSNBC.com

I am looking at a picture of a soldier aiming his
    M-16,
in a remote area of Afghanistan, where nearly
    half
of his platoon died, and he is being waved back,
    a retreat,
by two soldiers standing on the distant side
    of a wall,

while the eyes of this soldier fix on his sights,
    wide open,
and even though he may be trying to glance
    over
at the cameraman, who could have said to him,
    Give me
a quick pose before we get the hell out of here,
    I think

the soldier is doubtful, as uneasy as soldiers
    always are
when retreat is called, eyes fixed in fear that,
    while
the cameraman gets his once in a wartime picture
    of him,
the Taliban may get its once in a lifetime shot
    at him,

so is that his fear, or is it just a fear of this life?
    so fragile,
lost so quickly, that the cameraman shoots quickly,
    who just then
had to have this picture, just had to have it posted
    online.
The soldier is still as death, and only his eyes prove
    otherwise.

Sonnet for a Dead Crow

A dead crow fell at my feet as I walked
in this pestilent neighborhood. Rather
than check it out, I just assumed it ate
something off a lawn or swooped down
to check on a dead squirrel, when, *Bam!*
one of the children raised on video games
popped it with a BB or pellet gun; and even
though I know I'm supposed to report dead
birds to the authorities, since, well, they
may be carrying something, I stood there
like a buffoon, wondering if this were
an omen, that is, what would befall me next:
my heart turning off, a truck jumping the curb,
my life like a crazed video blinking, blinking.

After Reading a Novel Where the Women Fantasize about a Hunk on TV

So I ask myself, *Why is it that women don't fantasize*
        about me?

(as if they ever did) but, well, hope springs eternal,
        even

though the bedsprings don't anymore, and I suppose
        I need

not look any further than the purpuras, like flags
        waving

on my upper arms, or my huge bald spot flanked
        by hair

the color of catacombs, or the loss of height leaving
        me

without a neck, or, *Whoa*, that's enough to deter
        any

woman of whatever age from giving me a second
        look,

if, after a brief glance, she was kind enough to give
        a first look.

And so I say, *What about me as a person on the inside?*
        to which,

I suspect the answer might very well be, *Well what*
        about it?

BILLY STOREY

I am sleepless, in the middle of night, thinking
                    about
protesters in Wisconsin, about school teachers,
                    their right

to unions, and I am also thinking of when unions
                    began,
the abuses workers endured, both in and outside
                    mills or factories,

and how could America, the home of the free, let
                    it happen
in the first place, Depression or not, and now I am
                    wondering,

how many regulations protect workers compared
                    to then,
and to the rest of non-shop workers, whose welfare
                    is, yes,

still protected, to a point? and I remember Billy,
                    a nice kid
who worked, like most of my buddies, in a factory
                    after high school,

and when he broke the union line, he was beaten
                    so badly
he had to be hospitalized, Billy who never quarreled
                    his whole life

until then, who never threatened anyone, or raised
                    his fist
in anger, and yet was beaten to a pulp in front of the
                    Washington St.

plant of Fafnir Bearings, trying to cross a line that soon
                    after
disappeared, when industry in my town went South
                    big time.

Hey, Billy, you had more guts than the rest of us, our
                    red-haired friend,
soft in body but steeled in mind. I am proud to have
                    known you.

Würzburg in September

On my second day of a year-long stay in Würzburg,
                I am running,
with Jane and our eight-year-old twins, to catch
                a *Strassenbahn*
downtown and then for a leisurely tour of this
                walled city—
Sally and Wes in front, Jane next, and me trying
                to grab
onto the sleeve of her airy dress, just to hop on
                the *Strassenbahn*,

half-full, the driver indifferent to our efforts.
                Meanwhile,
Sally and Wes, who were dressed alike that day
                for
the last time, were charming the occupants,
                especially
the older women, even though no one understood
                anyone else,
while I fumbled at the front for the right amount
                to transport us

to the end of the line, which, I assumed wrongly,
                was not
where we boarded but in the far end of Würzburg,
                beyond
the walls, at a hospital where we exited unaware
                of where
we were, my reading knowledge of German proving
                to be
next to useless, and even though Würzburg housed
                our

Third Infantry Division, only a few natives spoke
                English;
and while Jane and I were trying to figure out how
                to get back
to our flat, a kind native spoke to us in English—
                his, as I recall,
as articulate as mine—saying, *Do you need assistance?*
                O Lord,
did we, the sun drooping over the *Festung Marienburg*
                in the distance,

    the kids hungry or tired, being eight, our clothes light
                for the cooling,
and I said in my crackled German, *Ya, Herr,* and that
                was
enough. He set us on the compass of our small world
                quickly.
Once back in our heated and more than ample flat,
                Jane and I
said to each other, *Hey we're going to love it here,*
                and we did.

Young Death in China

A two-year-old girl was hit by a van in China;
                      and while
the van stopped, no one got out, the van started
                      up, running
over her again, and more people noticed the girl
                      lying
in the street, but did nothing to remove her before
                      another

vehicle swerved but still hit her and did not stop,
                      nonetheless;
and I am trying to think, in the safe comfort
                      of my den,
how could this happen, and where else could
                      it happen—
raw, insensitive—and whatever adjectives I can
                      conjure up,

anywhere, and how can anyone leave a toddler,
                      now dead,
in the middle of a road and the people pass by her,
                      and I think
of why my late Jane never wanted to drive after
                      witnessing,
close up, when she was ten, a three-year old girl
                      run over

on Black Rock Avenue in New Britain, near home;
                      and like Jane
I will never forget what I saw distributed by Chinese
                      TV,
and I know Jane would have run out to the street,
                      picked
her up, and carried her, just carried her, wherever
                      she had to go.

A View from Here

Say you were sitting in my nearly vacant porch
        behind
a stand of lush fescue begging for your attention,
        not to cut,
but to admire, this being the season of the year
        it needs

to be cut every week, and behind it, sulking behind
        a low
stone wall, the world of the flood zone begins its
        own
nefarious life, snakes of whatever origin, patrolling
        the ditch,

and other creatures whose lives I am unable to
        identify,
as the waters rise, the drought easing, which is
        rare
so I am told, since I moved here, 10 years ago,
        when I never

saw or heard a bird or the same nervous antics
        of the legion
of squirrels that insist on nesting in our soffits
        or even worse,
in our attics, where they die, parasites feeding
        on them,

releasing ammonia in the air. How in such a short
        span
of time can a bucolic scene turn into a panorama
        of disease,
death, as it has, year after year, in Sub-Saharan
        Africa,

as in my waste zone in the back, where even
        the hardiest,
tough-skinned, woodsy guys are still reluctant
        to venture
into without the right protection for both body
        and mind?

Suppose the Return of Christ

So I'm thinking, perhaps irreverently, about why Christ
                  returned
in ways his disciples could not recognize him, as on
                  the road
to Emmaus, by the shore of the sea with fisherman,
                  elsewhere
too, and I keep wanting to ask *Why? Why did Christ
                  come back*

incognito? And suppose he were to return now—
                  in
what guise should we expect to find him? Maybe
                  as a broker
on Wall Street, a paramedic in the Sub-Saharan,
                  and, well,
how can we be sure it is Christ—because he says so?
                  If they could not

verify his person, how can we recognize him now?
                  Is it that God
prefers his son to be incognito, to check out the land,
                  so to speak,
and if so, what are we to do when the doubters feed
                  the media
with historical analogues, with controversies boiling
                  about Christ,

his authenticity, his redemptive quality; and what will
                  happen
to Christianity—perish in the textbooks of the world,
                  with Christ,
as a person, but what kind of a person, a good guy
                  or an agitator,
one whose journey, whose sufferings were justified,
                  or one

whose way goes the way of the steep four corners
                  of the Earth,
like a discounted theory of the origins of the universe,
                  and where
will we be then?—better off than now, in our beliefs,
                  or diminished,
our faith being rubbed out, as if by an eraser on a board
                  of history?

Last Letter to Jane

I am not sure how many times I said I would not
        bother you
again, and I know I am going back on my promise
        once more

and, perhaps, for no good reason, but after I took
        this
arcane test at the cardiologist's yesterday, they said
        my score

was not only abnormal but, far as I can understand,
        so off
the charts my heart could take a permanent vacation
        anytime,

which, well, made me think that maybe I should have
        another
stress test, as they wanted—them setting it up behind
        my back—

until I said, *No, not yet, I've got to think this through,*
        and then
I said to myself, in the quiet of my small office, *Uh oh,*
        this is

the big time, Ron, use your head, before there's nothing
        left,
and all the time I am thinking about you, your years of
        unbearable pain

and my pathetic attempts to make you feel better, and
        how
nervous and angry I became in the years when, No,
        you could not.

The Final Reading

At the final reading of my poems in this life,
                I will confess,
all the wrongs I have done, omitting none,
                including
even the time I changed a math answer in
                third grade

because I felt embarrassed for adding up
                poorly,
and I could never tell my parents my mistake.
                Soon after,
I began a guilt that found a warm home inside
                my head

all my life, like a bear in a geological fault,
                living out
its winters in a form of death, but not death,
                rather
a life-giving sleep, and that is what guilt must
                have been

for me then, until now, when I have to say,
                I confess,
and, of course, nobody cares what I had ever
                done or said,
believing none of it, knowing all along what
                liars

poets are, that they built lies like seawalls,
                bunkers,
storm cellars, but not to keep anything out,
                only to shelter
lies, to fabricate, to make up, to nurture them
                into poems.

The Last Poem
for JEM, 1938-2009

So now in the vast dimension of age
somewhere beyond the expanse of one's
imagining, I think of what could happen
and, hence, I can envision it as actual,
your loving me, teaching me how to love,
a lifeline that never drew down until
you died fifty years into the race, if not
a race, then a span of time in which I grew

out of my corduroy pants into, hey, loopy
khakis and jeans, at which time, I was also
in love with you, knowing of no rescue,
and, yes, we lived like that until the bells
chimed, and we both knew what the sound
meant and held each other tighter each day.

A Note on the Author

Ronald Moran was born in Philadelphia and moved to New Britain, Connecticut, when he was 10. He received his BA from Colby College and his MA and PhD from Louisiana State University. After having taught at the University of North Carolina for nine years, he joined the Clemson University faculty in 1975, and retired twice, first in 1998 and then in 2000. He served in a number of positions at Clemson, including Professor and Head of the Department of English, Associate Dean, and Interim Dean. In 1969-70, he was Fulbright Lecturer at the University of Würzburg in Germany. He has published twelve books/chapbooks of poetry, including *Saying These Things*, the inaugural volume of poetry issued by the Clemson University Digital Press in 2004. Moran is the author of one book of literary criticism and co-author of another. His poems and essays are widely published in magazines such as *Commonweal*, *Emrys Journal*, *Evening Street Review*, *The Louisiana Review*, *Mankato Poetry Review*, *North American Review*, *Northeast*, *Northwest Review*, *South Carolina Review*, *Southern Review*, *Tar River Poetry*, and *Yankee*. Moran lives in Simpsonville, South Carolina. His work is archived in the James B. Duke Library at Furman University, and he has won numerous awards for his poetry.

www.ingramcontent.com/pod-product-compliance
Lightning Source LLC
Chambersburg PA
CBHW031125160426
43192CB00008B/1112